IMAGINAIRE
The Magic 7
Contemporary Magic Realism

www.fantasmus.com

FANTASMUS ARTBOOKS PRESENTS
THE IMAGINAIRE SERIES

IMAGINAIRE VIII
Release date Fall 2015
Guest of honour: Michael Maschka - Germany

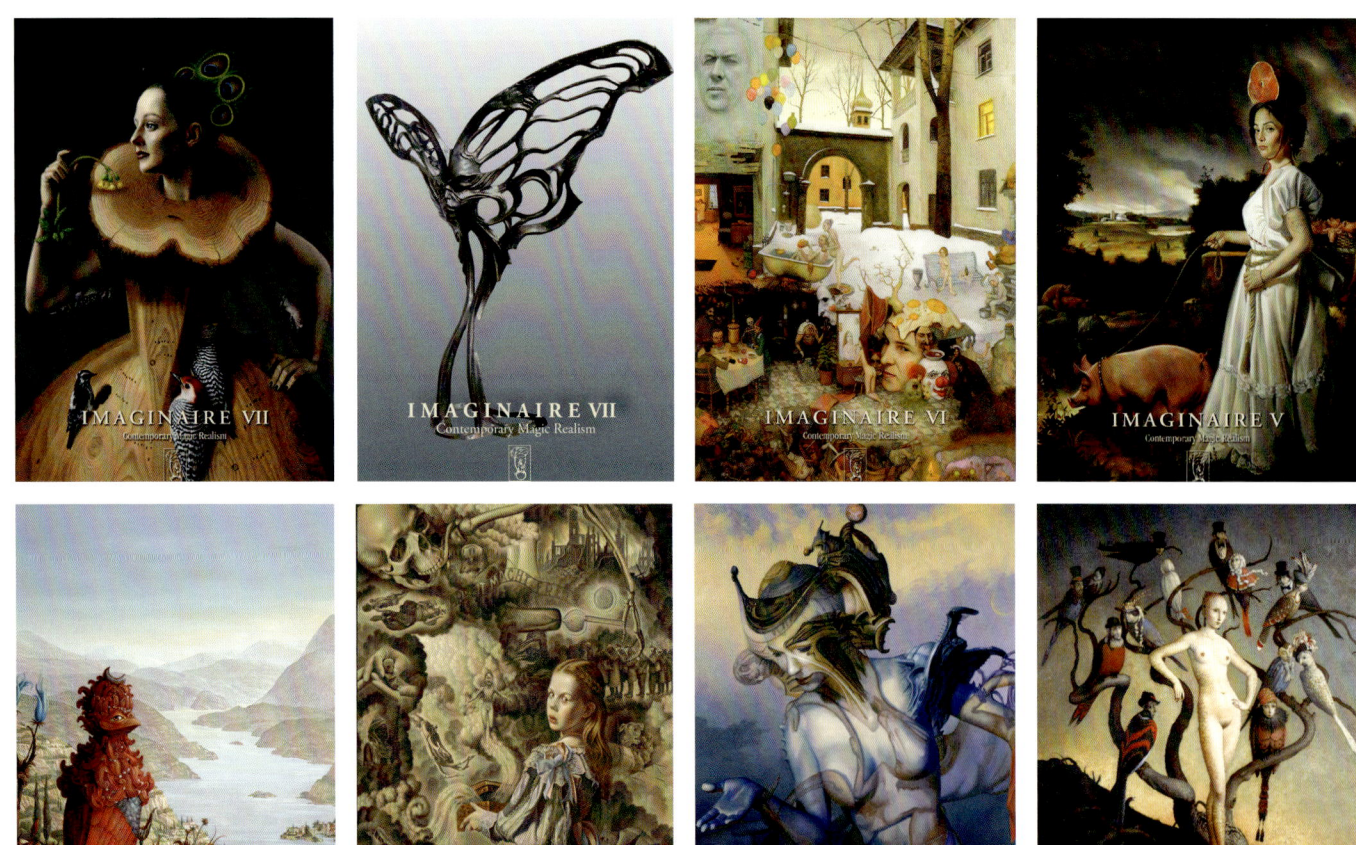

Check at www.fantasmus.com for this and many more books and events!

INDEX PAINTERS

Page 4
INTRODUCTION - by Claus Brusen
Page 6
FANTASMUS - Since then, Now, Coming up

Page 8
STEVEN KENNY - GUEST OF HONOUR
Page 28
ALAYNE ABRAHAMS
Page 30
KAROL BAK
Page 34
ELVIRA BARANOVA
Page 38
DAVID MICHAEL BOWERS
Page 42
GERT BRASQUE
Page 44
CLAUS BRUSEN
Page 50
GIL BRUVEL
Page 52
RONALD BURNS
Page 54
VAL DYSHLOV
Page 56
MONICA FAGAN
Page 58
N.G.HAMMER
Page 60
BJØRN HAUGAARD
Page 62
MICHAEL HIEP
Page 64
JOSEPH KALIHER
Page 68
RICK LELIEVELD
Page 72
PATRICK VAN DER LINDE

Page 74
THOR LINDENEG
Page 76
JACK LIPOWCZAN
Page 80
MICHA LOBI
Page 86
LUDMILA
Page 88
GINNY PAGE
Page 90
JOSE PARRA
Page 92
GRASZKA PAULSKA
Page 94
JULIANA PAVLOVA
Page 96
JUERGEN PLEIKIES
Page 98
DAG SAMSUND
Page 100
ISKREN SEMKOV
Page 102
HERMAN SMORENBURG
Page 104
TEGNER BRUNO
Page 106
JEAN THOMASSEN
Page 112
TWEEKUNST
Page 114
CLAUDE VERLINDE
Page 116
CAS WATERMAN
Page 118
STIG WEYE
Page 120
DIRKJE WIGARDA
Page 122
SIEGFRIED ZADEMACK

INTRODUCTION

I assume we can make it clear that crises is over, we now have to call it a permanent situation. We have to rebuild what was lost during the past 7 years. Befor the financial crises the Fantastic art had a firm grib in people, we had more and more attention on our exhibitions and books, we still have and it is still growing, what we have missed is sale. Sale are picking up slowly, but I doubt if we shall, ever see times like we have up till the crises started and perhaps this is fine, we had a period where almost everything was possible without critisism and in order to make a stand at the art scene, we need to be critical, we need to be good in sorting out in quality and I believe this has also happened.
We can each and every one of only do what we consider best and together this will make a difference.

Guests of honour are Steven Kenny and Igor Grechanyk

"The Birdman". Steven Kenny was one of the first foreign artists I became friends with back in 2003, Kenny was such a very gentle person, from the beginning we started communicated as if we had known eachother since forever. The unique style of technic used by Kenny is similar to the old school of Italy and his choice of subject is always something with birds, which is why I chose to call him "The Birdman". I think you can only count on 2 hands paintings done without a feather throughout his career. Kenny recently moved to St. Petersburg with his wife Diohn, he of course became involved with the St. Petersburg Dali museum of Mr. & Mrs Reynold Morse, where he has become a tourguide.
Kenny has also worked for some years as a Commercial Illustrator on various projects, among those, a number of album covers for the American band Journey.

Igor Grechanyk, Ukrainian sculptur. Grechanyk always make his sculpture unique, not one has been done in more than one copy. Grechanyk has made a lot of monumental sculptures for his homecountry Ukraine all no matter size handmade to the smallest detail, nothing escapes his eye for the finish of his work. I have known Grechanyk since 2005 as I was working with Galerie Michelle Boulet in Paris, she had found this new Ukraine artist she wanted me to see, so when I was invited to participate in a group exhibition in Nice at Galerie Princesse de Kiev, what was more naturel than asking the Galerie to invite Grechanyk from Kiev, This was where we meet the first time in February 2007. We have kept contact ever since and we always have a number of sculptures for exhibitions present at Fantasmus.

It is a first time we do a double cover version of IMAGINAIRE, you just flip the book and chose between Sculptures or Painters. We decided to make this special as we call it the Magic Seven, seven is a magic number in both mythology and in religion, so we decided to celebrate this instead of the usual of 5, 10 or 15 years. We chose to make this a 7, 9 and 13 where we will make something different.

ART BOOKS since last IMAGINAIRE:

COSM has made a journal vol 8. This is more about their spiritual society rather than an artbook, but a lot of fine artists are connected to this organisation, it is a fine series to collect if you have interest in the more Visionary and Spiritual art. It is possible to buy at their webshop http://shop.cosm.org along with other items, such as poster, t-shirts ect, ect.

I was sent this fine book by Dorian Vallejo, son of famous artist couple Julie Bell and Boris Vallejo, but with this book I can say that Dorian does not stand in the shadow of his parents, he is a full grown artists with his very own touch, in some way far from his parents work, but what they have in commen is the facination of the human body, I must admit, Dorian is far better but this is my personal oppinion. This book can be bought at hi webpage http://dorianvallejo.com/book/ it is possible to buy a collectors book, it comes with an original drawing inside the book, well worth spending the extra money on.

Off course again, the Fenners have made vol: 21 Spectrum, a showcase of Commercial fantastic fine art and comic art.

Feast of Consequence, Musical project by Fish and Mark Wilkinson, this unique book and CD by Fish (ex. Marillion) and Mark Wilkinson, commercial illustrator/artist. has just before we go to printing, won the Storm Thorgerson Grand Design Award at @ProgMagazineUK awards 2014 in London. We can proudly say that we at FANTASMUS published Mark Wilkinson's monography Shadowplay.
Feast of Consequence is a beautiful book with mainly digital art, but Mark is also a very skilled AirBrush artist, most of the work in the book is mixed media and I will not forget to mention that Julie Wilkinson, Marks wife and partner has done a lot of the work in the book too, she is actually too a very skilled artist, but spend most of her time assisting Mark with his work.

Claus Brusen, October 2014

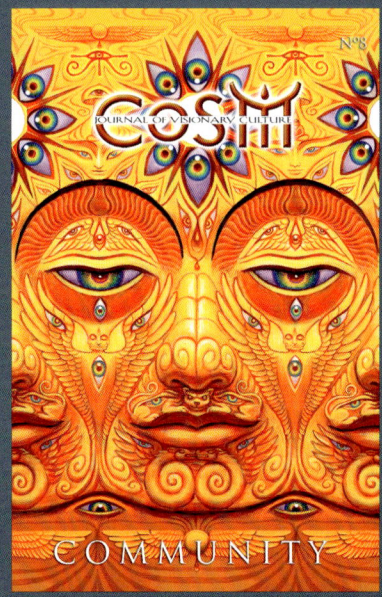
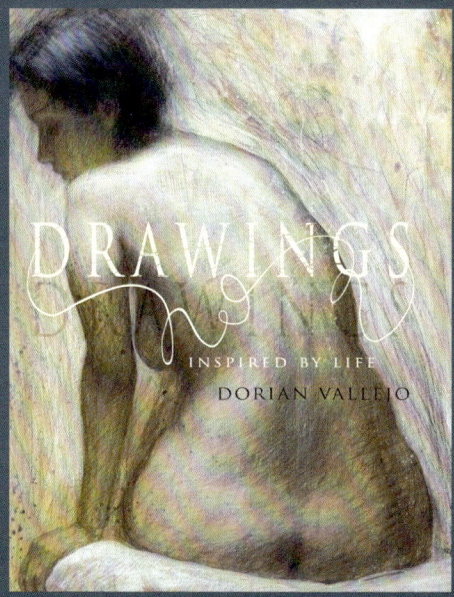

FANTASMUS
Since then - Now - Coming up

Many things have happened since the last edition of IMAGINAIRE. We've had a very well visited exhibition in FANTASMUS when we had the book launch of IMAGINAIRE VI in which Micha Lobi was the guest of honour. The main part of the artists in the book was represented and at the opening we had a special visit from 3 ambassadeurs. From Ukraine, Bulgaria and Armenia. 6 weeks later we had our annual erotic christmas show which was delightful as usual
During Easter we had a 2-man-show as we had Tim Roosens Roboville Robots along with Claus Brusens world of Nactalius. A popular and humorous exhibition that appealed to both children and grown-ups.

During summer we relocated and got a new and permanent residence for FANTASMUS. We've had the luck of moving into and old house in beautiful surroundings in Roskilde Fjord and as a part of Selsoe and Lindholm Castle. This has been a blessing as the Baron and owner of the castles has invited us to use his privatee castle for the presentation og this years IMAGINAIRE book and exhibition. We are looking forward to this as those surrounding fit this beautiful art perfectly.

An ongoing proces is the FANTASMUS Trust which has been established. We are proud to say that 10 artists have given the trust a present in shape of painting in the size 30 x 30 cm which are going to be on permanent display in FANTASMUS and of course in the museum when it becomes a reality. Thank you for believing in us and for the wonderful paintings you have donated!

This time it is not only IMAGINAIRE that we proudly can present in FANTASMUS. We also have the pleasure of launching the first book in a new series in FANTASMUS that present specific artists. This time it is about Claus Brusen. For all artists interested just get in touch with us in FANTASMUS.

Last, but not least, I would like to thank both Igor Grechanyk and Steven Kenny for contributing in this edition of IMAGINAIRE. We are proud to have these two guests of honour in this special edition of IMAGINAIRE - The Magic 7. Of course a thank you to all our paticipating artists. Without you this wouldn't happen. Enjoy this edition of IMAGINAIRE and keep supporting the genre.

Mette Torp Bisgaard, October 2014

STEVEN KENNY
1962 USA
www.stevenkenny.com

When we are born, our world is made up of an unfiltered stream of external and internal stimuli. Before a certain age we make no distinctions between touch, sight, smell, sound, taste, emotion30

Figurative painting dates back about 30,000 years. Among the drawings on the walls of the Lascaux caves in France is a depiction of a bird-headed human figure --- a shaman with the ability to transcend space and time and act as an intermediary between the earth and spirit. This idea of bridging terrestrial and celestial realms has been with us in various forms ever since.

Thankfully, there is a flourishing group of artists working today --- the Magic Realists --- who give free rein to their reveries and manifest them in their work. These artists keep alive a creative tradition that stretches back to the birth of humankind. Actually, until the invention of photography, artists relied more heavily on their imaginations and less on accurately copying the visual world around them. For example, during the Renaissance, Leonardo da Vinci encouraged his students to quiet their minds and stare at random patterns on plaster walls or knotty wood grain, ashes, clouds, etc. He knew that with the help of the unconscious mind, images begin to emerge to form the basis of fantastic visions beyond the scope of what the conscious mind might conjure on its own. More than 400 years later, with the help of Sigmund Freud's psychoanalytic discoveries, Salvador Dali coined the term Paranoic-critical Method to describe his early Surrealist process. Dali would intentionally dredge up images from the depths of his unconscious, manifesting themselves uncensored in his imagination. He would then consciously edit them to create the subjects for his paintings. Some years later, the psychologist Carl Jung coined the term "active imagination" to describe the amplification, interpretation and integration of images found in dreams and works of art.

At a very young age, unaware that I was following a well-worn artistic path, I fell into using these creative methods. I delighted in sitting quietly, tapping into my imagination, allowing wondrous images to rise freely and materialize in my mind. This process seemed only natural to me at the time. As an artist, I've never found satisfaction in simply reproducing what my eyes see before me. Instead, my interest has always laid in juxtaposing seemingly unrelated images to create dreamlike scenes that, to me, carried so much more power and significance than straightforward still lifes, landscapes or portraits.

It can be said that the imagination mediates between human reason and divine inspiration. The trained imagination can access and inhabit that zone between the sensory and the spiritual planes, between the mind and the soul, the head and the heart. If we agree that our thoughts, feelings, actions and world view are deeply influenced by the power of our unconscious minds, then true reality must exist somewhere in that fluid space between inner and outer realities; a blending of both.

In that sense, Magic Realism may provide us with the most honest and transparent representation of the world as we experience it. By visually articulating our impression of the world in ways that allow our unconscious minds to fill in the gaps, make connections, and complete the picture, we engage all our resources and faculties --- mind, heart and soul. This is why I feel the Magic Realist movement is so essential and I am proud to call myself a member of this vital genre.

Steven Kenny, 2014

Right page: The Gift · 2007 ·76,2 x 50,8 cm · Oil on linen

Bubbles · 71,1 x 91,4 cm · Oil on canvas

The Saplings · 81,3 x 61 cm · Oil on linen

Earthborn · 76,2 x 61 cm · Oil on linen

10 IMAGINAIRE VII

Leda and the Swan · 91,4 x 121,9 cm · Oil on canvas

The Stump · 45,7 x 61 cm · Oil on panel

IMAGINAIRE VII

The Release · 96,5 x 66 cm · Oil on linen

Winterlude · 127 x 76,2 cm · Oil on linen

The Braid · 61 x 45,7 cm · Oil on canvas

The Perch IV · 50,8 x 40,6 cm · Oil on panel

Left page: Moondance · 50,8 x 40,6 cm · Oil on linen

The Veil · 61 x 81,3 cm · Oil on linen

IMAGINAIRE VII

Death before Birth · 97 x 61 cm · Oil on linen

The Law of Gravity · 61 x 45,7 cm · Oil on panel

The Surrender · 66 x 66 cm · Oil on canvas

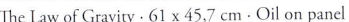

The Return to Eden · 50,8 x 61 cm · Oil on panel

IMAGINAIRE VII 17

The Decoy · 61 x 91,4 cm · Oil on linen

The Attendant · 76,2 x 91,4 cm · Oil on canvas

18 IMAGINAIRE VII

The Pinnacle · 101,6 x 66 cm · Oil on canvas

The Crux II · 55,9 x 152,4 cm · Oil on linen

The Reins · 61 x 86,4 cm · Oil on linen

The Island · 121,9 x 91,4 cm · Oil on canvas

Left page: The Rain Gown · 81,3 x 61 cm · Oil on linen

The Rescue · 96,5 x 61 cm · Oil on linen

IMAGINAIRE VII

The Wing · 101,6 x 76,2 cm · Oil on canvas

The Butterfly · 51 x 41 cm · Oil on panel

The Prince · 91,4 x 61 cm · Oil on linen

The Bark Necklace · 61 x 45,7 cm · Oil on panel

Tethered Fulcrum · 40,6 x 101,6 cm · Oil on linen

The Ruff · 66 x 61 cm · Oil on canvas

IMAGINAIRE VII

The Lantern · 76,2 x 61 cm · Oil on linen

The Imposter · 76,2 x 55,9 cm · Oil on linen

IMAGINAIRE VII

ALAYNE ABRAHAMS
1953 USA
www.alayneabrahams.com

Detail: The Mask · Watercolour on paper

Musings of Mucha · 35,6 x 50,8 cm · Watercolour on paper

The Mask · 35,6 x 50,8 cm · Watercolour on paper

IMAGINAIRE VII

KAROL BAK

1961 Poland
www.karolbak.com

Miss Fortuna · 100 x 100 cm · Oil on canvas

Prima Mobilia XIV · 46 x 46 cm · Oil on panel

Time XIII · 100 x 100 cm · Oil on panel

Glamour · 100 x 100 cm · Oil on canvas

Prima Mobilia · 50 x 100 cm · Oil on canvas

Starlight · 100 x 100 cm · Oil on canvas

IMAGINAIRE VII

Prima Mobilia XLII · 50 x 50 cm · Oil on canvas

Aurora · 60 x 60 cm · Oil on canvas

Time · 100 x 100 cm · Oil on canvas

Page 39: Dawn · 100 x 81 cm · Oil on canvas

ELVIRA BARANOVA
New Zealand
www.elviraart.com

Moonlight Melody · 61 x 61 cm · Oil/acrylic on Canvas

Spirit of Blue Fish · 31 x 41 cm · Oil/acrylic on Canvas

Twilight Warrior · 76 x 76 cm · Oil/acrylic on Canvas

IMAGINAIRE VII 35

Queen of Destiny · 76 x 61 cm · Oil/acrylic on canvas

Dreaming of Venice · 51 x 51 cm · Oil/acrylic on canvas

Masquerade of Angels · Triptych 3 x 31 x 61 cm · Oil/acrylic on canvas

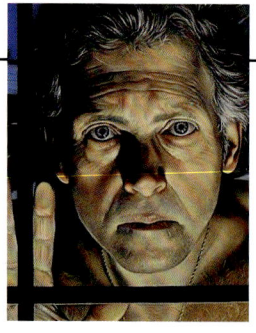

DAVID MICHAEL BOWERS
1956 USA
www.dmbowers.com

The Girl in the Blue Kimono · 76,2 x 101,6 cm · Oil on linen

Finding the Gold · 86,4 x 61 cm · Oil on linen

Detail: Finding the Gold · 86,4 x 61 cm · Oil on linen

Detail: Reflections · 61 x 45,7 cm · Oil on panel

Ship of Fools · 61 x 86,4 cm · Oil on linen

40 IMAGINAIRE VII

Reflections · 61 x 45,7 cm · Oil on panel

GERT BRASQUE
1946 Denmark
www.gertbrask.dk

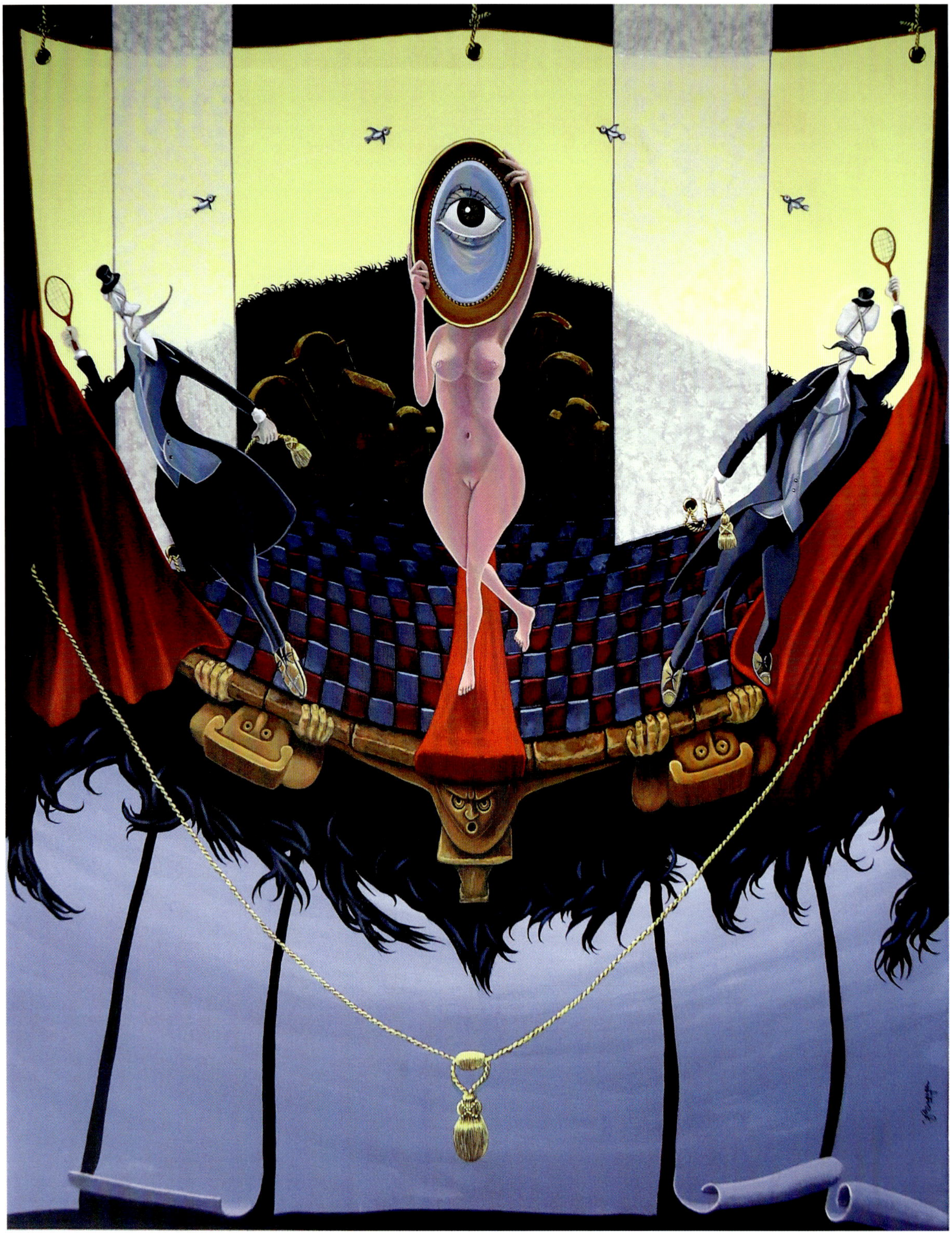

Oh (how I miss) those Victorian Evenings · 100 x 80 cm · Acrylic on canvas

To mand frem for en enke · 50 x 50 cm · Acrylic on canvas

Dansemesteren · 50 x 50 cm · Acrylic on canvas

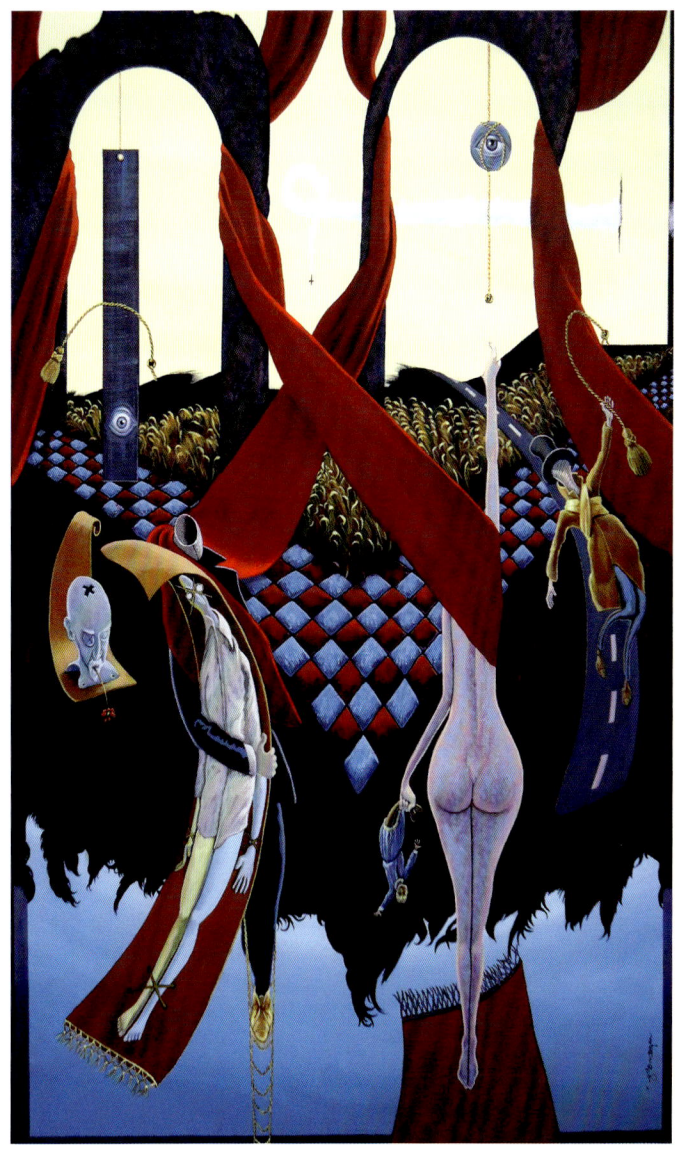
Goodmorning Sunshine · 100 x 70 cm · Acrylic on canvas

Optræk til noget · 50 x 30 cm · Acrylic on canvas

IMAGINAIRE VII 43

CLAUS BRUSEN
1960 Denmark
www.clausbrusen.com

Small Talk II · 27 x 22 cm · Oil on panel

King Toad at his Court with the captured Fairy · 40 x 30 cm · Oil on panel

The Good, The Bad and The Ugly · 27 x 22 cm · Oil on panel

Eruption · 40 x 30 cm · Oil on panel

Flying to the Land of Makebelieve · 55 x 75 cm · Oil on panel

46 IMAGINAIRE VII

The Question · 40 x 30 cm · Oil on panel

The Guardian Owl of Nactalius · 24 x 18 cm · Oil on panel

48 IMAGINAIRE VII

Tegner Bruno · 50 x 40 cm · Oil on panel

The Cubist Series

Each of the innumerable components that make up who I am is unrecognizable on its own: a childhood memory of morning sunlight striking the corner of a neighboring roof; my body's plasma and cells; subatomic structures; energy waves. In this instant, all the parts converge. Something seamless and infinitely complex is formed, something that could not exist until this moment, and that will change again in indescribable ways a moment from now. Yet somehow it remains whole.

The light touches my face on just this angle, right now, and precisely at the same angle it touches this thought, this tuft of grass by my feet, that skyline, the delicate hair on my arm. Whatever unseen force moves beneath the surface of everything has choreographed the dance of continuous emergence to create what I am—and what I am is intrinsically, rhythmically, intertwined with what we all are.

Gussie Fauntleroy

GIL BRUVEL
1959 USA
www.bruvel.com

Journey Series # 4

The companionable forest undulates in deep-blue serenity—primordial, alive, sharing the journey with the animals and child. In this permeable realm of childhood dreams, of memory before memory, they travel together like family. Quietly, comfortably, they stride through the familiar into the unknown, as flora and sky dissolve into waves and particles of energy: the quantum cartwheel of possibility and choice. In awakened life, as well, child and elephant walk within the same dreams, toward the same fate. What befalls one, befalls the other equally; what one deserves, the other as deeply deserves. The pivotal moment is now. Neither animal nor human needs any justification but this: to be.

Watching the moon at dawn, solitary, mid-sky, I knew myself completely: no part left out. - Izimu Shikibu
    or
We have forgotten what rocks, plants, and animals still know. We have forgotten how to be—to be still, to be ourselves, to be where life is: Here and now. - Eckhart Tolle

Scent # 2

If scent is color is energy, feeling and form, how does this radiance meet the world? It vibrates out from a peaceful core. It grows deep inside like tendrils of spring, like layers unfolding, like passages surging open to release the vital fragrance of life. It shimmers in rainbow hues as is passes through the periphery of her soul. It streams like excitement from her curious, irrepressible mind. It melts in waves from her confident presence, changing all it touches in subtle yet powerful ways. She is woman as the world has known her forever—and also as the world has never seen.

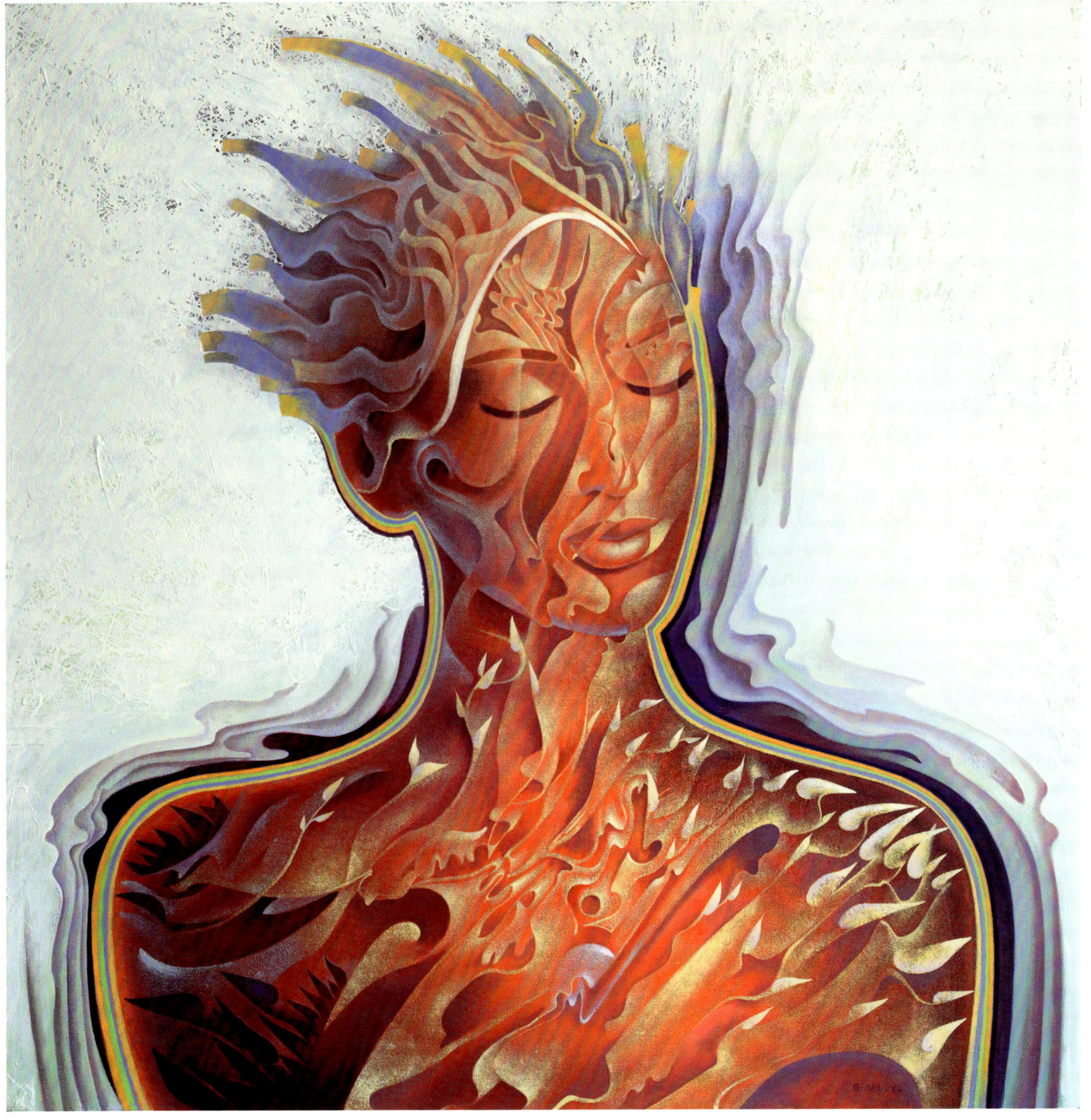

RONALD BURNS
1942 Denmark
www.ronaldburns.dk

No title · 50x 65 cm · Pencil and watercolour

No title · 65 x 100 cm · Pencil and watercolour

No title · 65 x 100 cm · Pencil and ink

IMAGINAIRE VII 53

VAL DYSHLOV
1950 USA
www.valdyshlov.com

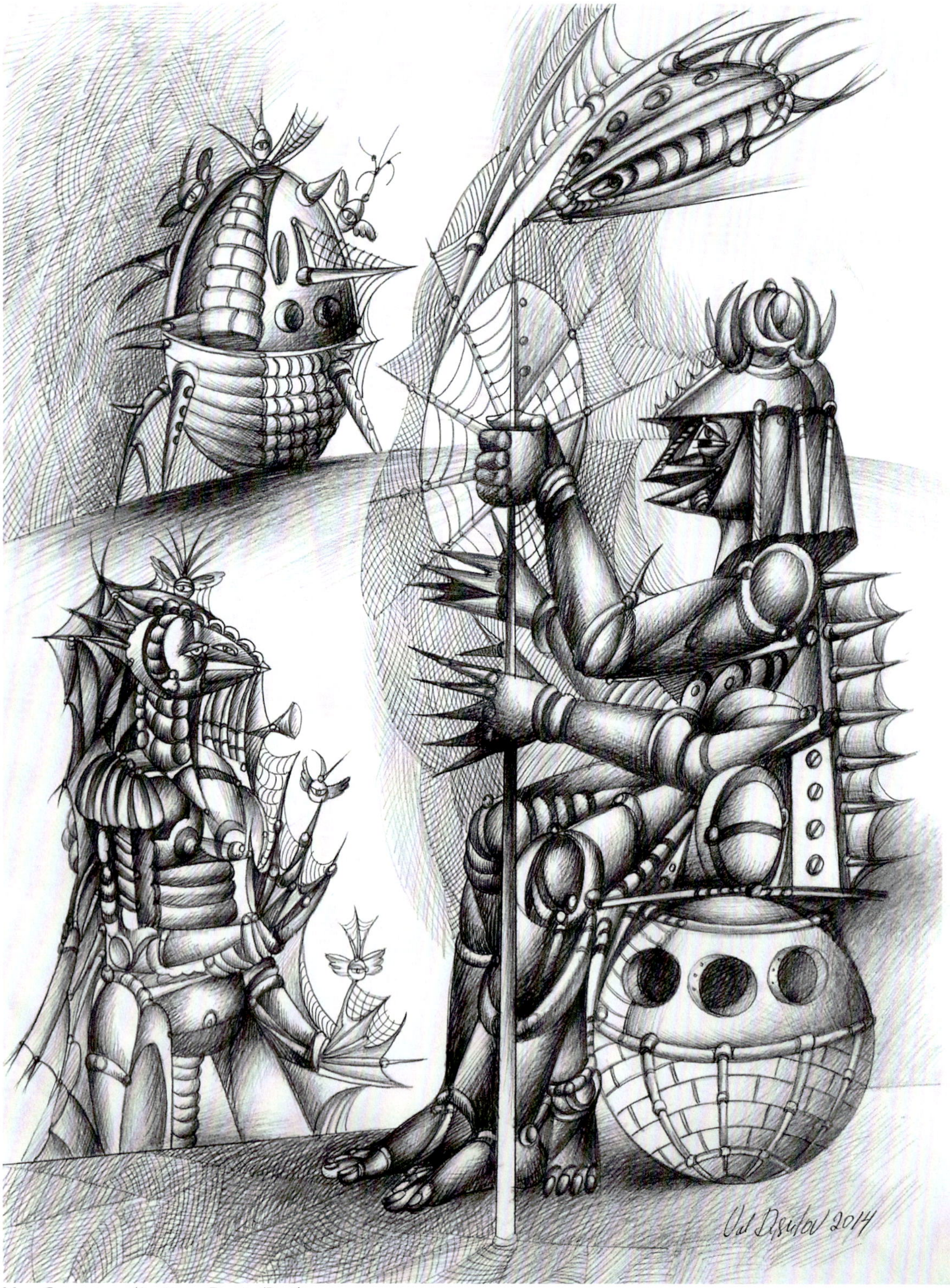

Merry Companions · 43 x 33 cm · Drawing/Pencil on paper

Confrontation · 43 x 33 cm · Drawing/Pencil on paper

Escalation · 43 x 33 cm · Drawing/Pencil on paper

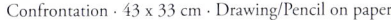

Element · 43 x 33 cm · Drawing/Pencil on paper

IMAGINAIRE VII 55

MONICA FAGAN
England
www.monica-fagan.com

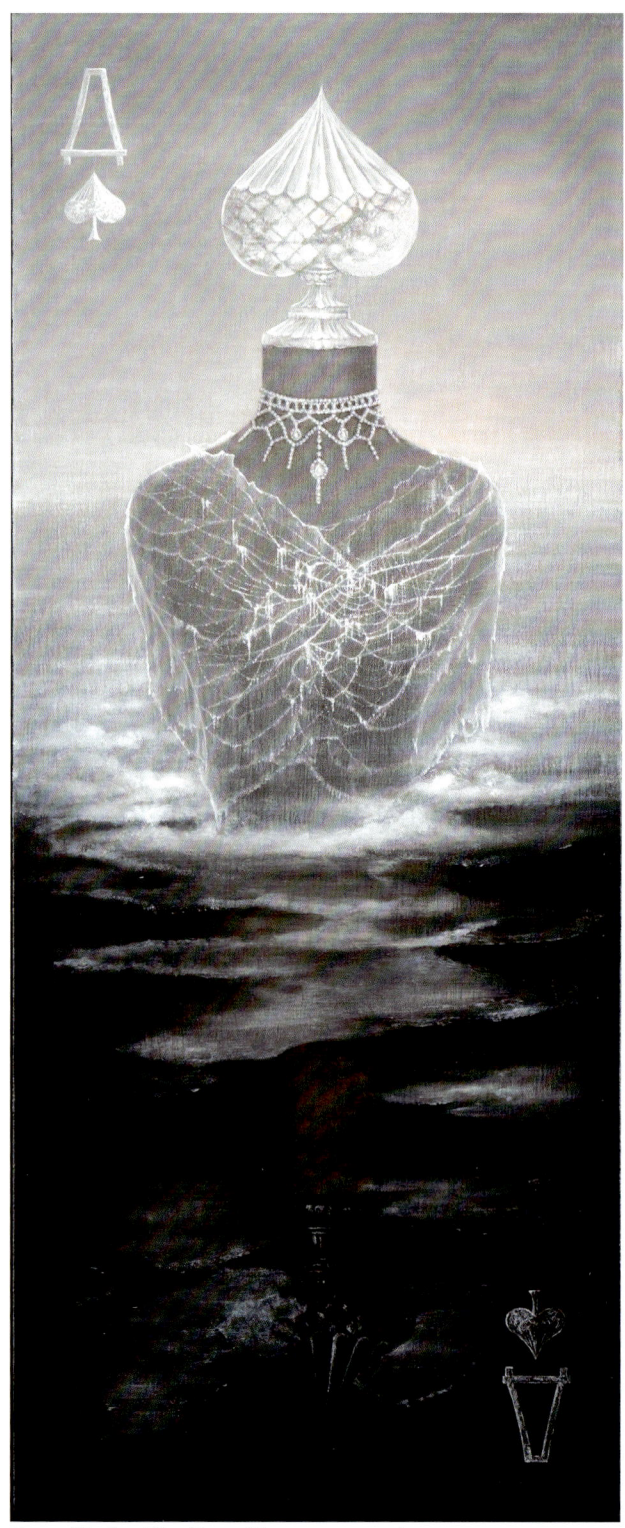

Queen of Spades · 100 x 42 cm · Oil on canvas on wood

Tosca· 100 x 42 cm · Oil on canvas on wood

Diva · 146 x 114 cm · Oil on canvas

N.G.HAMMER
1964 Sweden/Denmark
www.nghammer.com

No title - Oil on canvas

No title - Oil on canvas

BJØRN HAUGAARD
1960 Denmark
www.123hjemmeside.dk/bjoernhaugaard

The glorious moment in time, when "Überschwein" freed his mind, and rose above the mob · 80 x 60 cm · Oil on canvas

Time Out · 50 x 50 cm · Oil on canvas

As Time Goes By · 100 x 150 cm · Oil on canvas

IMAGINAIRE VII

MICHAEL HIEP
1959 The Netherlands
www.michaelhiep.nl

Sleeping Beauty and the Wheel of Samsara · 120 x 90 cm · Oil on canvas

The Temptation of Snow White · 120 x 90 cm · Oil on canvas

JOSEPH KALIHER

1970 Italy/USA

www.jwk.altervista.org

Picnic within The Magic Wood of Venus · 50 x 40 cm · Oil on canvas

We Are all sons of a fusion into The One..Supreme Being! · 150 x 100 cm · Oil on canvas

Staying Afloat · 30 x 40 cm · Oil on canvas

The walk yonder vanity · 100 x 70 cm · Oil on canvas

Freudian reflections upon my anal stepmother · 80 x 60 cm · Oil on canvas

RICK LELIEVELD

1963 The Netherlands
www.rick-lelieveld.nl

It's all between the ears · 75 x 75 cm · Oil on panel

Dancing water · 80 x 80 cm · Oil on panel

Sweet Dreams · 75 x 75 cm · Oil on panel

Fertility · 60 x 80 cm · Oil on panel

70 IMAGINAIRE VII

Sweet Dreams · detail

Temptation · 80 x 80 cm · Oil on panel

See no evil, hear no evil · 80 x 96 cm · Oil on panel

IMAGINAIRE VII 71

PATRICK VAN DER LINDE

1972 The Netherlands
www.patrickvanderlinde.nl

Rebuilding · 55 x 70 cm · Oil on canvas

Through the Jungle · 50 x 110 cm · Oil on canvas

And the winner is..... · 50 x 70 cm · Oil on canvas

THOR LINDENEG
1941 Denmark
www.lindeneg.dk

Allegori · 80 x 80 cm · Oil on canvas

Nature Morte · 80 x 80 cm · Oil on canvas

Summer · 80 x 80 cm · Oil on canvas

JACK LIPOWCZAN

1951 Poland/Germany
www.jali-art.com

Small Talk.... · 65 x 50 cm · Oil on wood

Merry Widov · 65 x 50 cm · Oil on wood

And how to live, Premier Minister? · 65 x 50 cm · Oil on wood

No gender - Blessed House Retreat · 50 x 65 cm · Oil on wood

IMAGINAIRE VII

Three Beauties · 65 x 50 cm · Oil on wood

Heart Breaker · 65 x 50 cm · Oil on wood

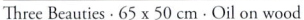

Heart Breaker · 50 x 65 cm · Oil on wood

78　IMAGINAIRE VII

Cycle Emigrants - Wainting for the News at the Wunderplatz · 50 x 65 cm · Oil on wood

Politician Dolce Vita · 50 x 65 cm · Oil on wood

IMAGINAIRE VII 79

MICHA LOBI

1967 Russia
www.fantasmus.com
m.lobi@mail.ru

House on the Edge · 15 x 14 cm · Oil on panel

Lunch · 20 x 33 cm · Oil on panel

Sisters of Mercy · 17 x 21 cm · Oil on panel

The Temptation of St. Antonius 1 · 30 x 42 cm · Oil and tempera on panel

The Orient Chamber · 20 x 30 cm · Oil and tempera on panel

Temptation of St. Anthony · 34,5 x 74 cm · Oil and tempera on panel

Meal of the Fool · 38 x 36 cm · Oil and tempera on panel

IMAGINAIRE VII

Forgotten Village · 42 x 61,5 cm · Oil and tempera on panel

On the Summer Ice · 65 x 77 cm · Oil and tempera on panel

84 IMAGINAIRE VII

Red Wine · 17,5 x 34 cm · Oil and tempera on panel

On the River · 14 x 18 cm · Oil on panel

IMAGINAIRE VII 85

LUDMILA
1958 Russia/Portugal
www.ludmila-fantasticart.blogspot.com

The Portrait of the Horse · 62 x 62 cm · Oil on panel

Nomad Princess · 33 x 41 cm · Oil on canvas

Hunter · 30 x 30 cm · Oil on canvas

GINNY PAGE
1963 England/Denmark
www.ginnypage.dk

Time to reflect · 127 x 95 cm · Oil on canvas

This is not a bowl of cherries · 60 x 78 cm · Oil on canvas

Still life with lemons and bees · 60 x 78 cm · Oil on canvas

Victoria with blue anemones · 127 x 95 cm · Oil on canvas

Needle and the Damage · 35 x 51 cm · Oil on canvas

IMAGINAIRE VII 89

JOSÉ PARRA
1975 Mexico
www.joseparra.com

Blue Bird · 50 x 70 cm · Oil on canvas

The Last Ships · 100 x 150 cm · Oil on canvas

The Ship of Fools · 195 x 130 cm · Oil on canvas

GRASZKA PAULSKA

Poland
www.grazapp.devianart.com

No title · 57 x 70 cm · Oil on panel

No title · 70 x 57 cm · Pastel on panel

JULIANA PAVLOVA

1968 Bulgaria
www.jutopia.me

Pray · 100 x 70 cm · acrylic on metal foil

Music and Soul · 70 x 100 cm · acrylic on metal foil

Me · 70 x 100 cm · mixed media on canvas

JUERGEN PLEIKIES

1944 Germany
www.atelier-pleikies.de

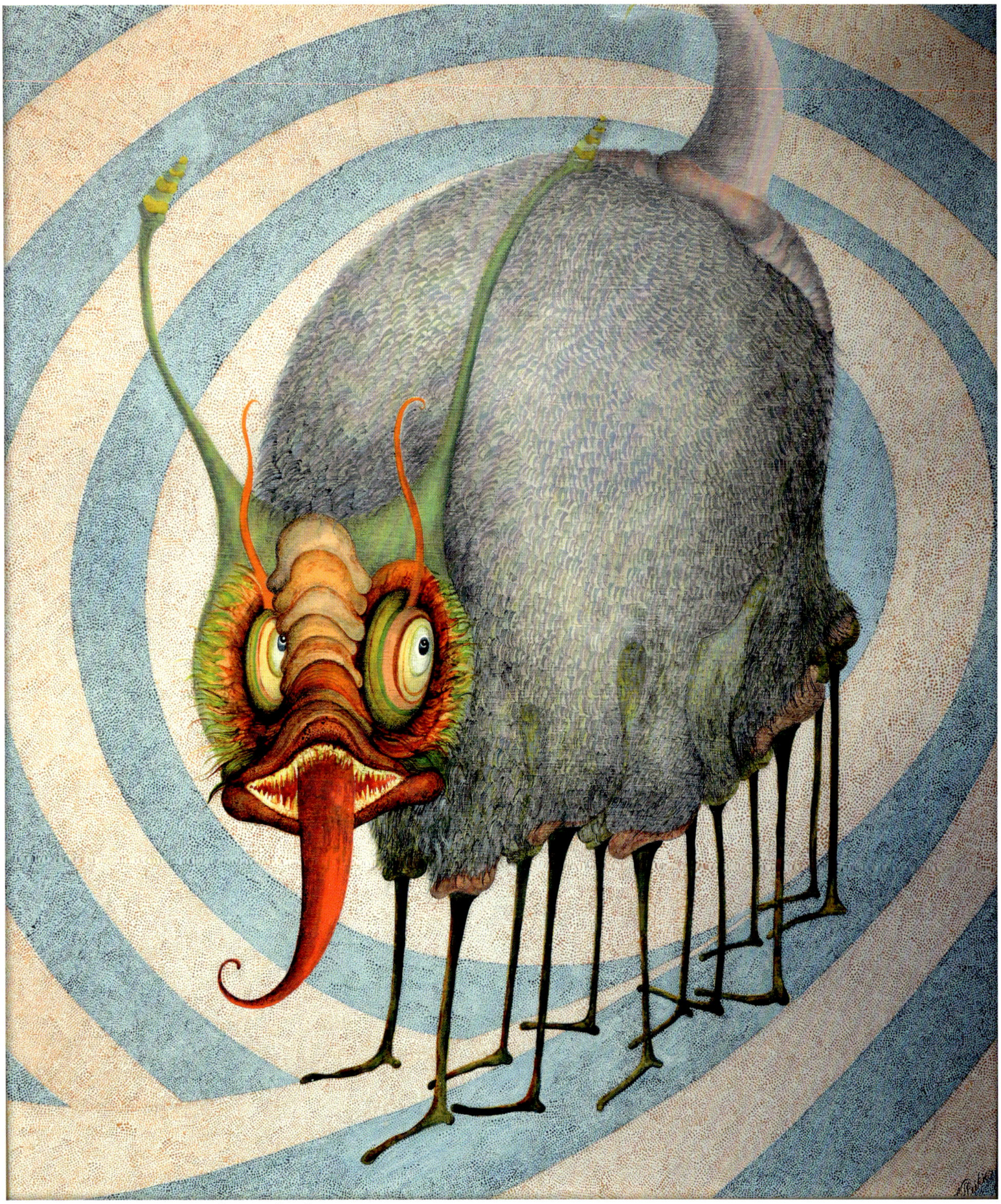

Visit to the 3 D · 130 x 112 cm · Acrylic on cardboard

Life #1 · 100 x 70 cm · Crayon

DAG SAMSUND
1949 Denmark
www.art-samsund.dk

Magnolia · 120 x 120 cm · Tempera and acrylics on canvas

Love in the lake · 15 x 21 cm · Tempera and oil on panel

Sisters · 40 x 40 cm · Acrylics on panel

Flying Balls · 80 x 80 cm · Tempera and oil on panel

IMAGINAIRE VII 99

ISKREN SEMKOV
1984 Bulgaria/Switzerland
www.iskrensemkov.com

Spring Messenger · 46 x 30 cm · Oil on canvas

Urban Still Life I · 25 x 25 cm - Oil on canvas

Urban Still Life II · 25 x 25 cm - Oil on canvas

Time Travelers · 20 x 20 cm - Oil on canvas

Beyond · 20 x 20 cm - Oil on canvas

The Nest · 22 x 22 cm - Oil on canvas

Mother of Wisdom · 30 x 30 cm - Oil on canvas

IMAGINAIRE VII

HERMAN SMORENBURG
1958 The Netherlands
www.hermansmorenburg.com

Whispers from Eternity · 80 x 60 cm · Oil on panel

Liberation · 73 x 118 cm - Oil on panel

Mysteries of the Sea · 50 x 60 cm - Oil on panel

TEGNER BRUNO
1959 Denmark
www.tegnerbruno.dk

Euterpe · 89 x 70 cm · Pen and acrylic on canvas

Professor Adelart Antoni and Miss Melusine Olsson flying his Flamboyant Combinationballoon · 82 x 112 cm · Pen, watercolor & acrylic on paper

Professor Adelart Antony Flying over the Alps in Merry Weather · 70 x 90 cm · Pen & acrylic on canvas

IMAGINAIRE VII 105

JEAN THOMASSEN
1949 The Netherlands
www.jeanthomassen.nl

9-11 · 60 x 50 cm · Oil on panel

Portrait of Mr. Glenn Janes · 90 x 70 cm · Oil on canvas

Redlight district of Amsterdam · 60 cm x 50 cm · Oil on canvas

Skitzo's are coming · 24 x 18 cm · Oil on canvas

Heaven, left part of the tryptic Last Judgementday · 90 cm x 60 cm · Oil on panel

Hell, right part of the tryptic Last Judgementday · 90 x 60 cm · Oil on panel

Andy Summers, Anne-Fieke Later and Eugène Later

TWEEKUNST
The Netherlands
www.tweekunst.nl

The Tobias symphony part 1 & 2

In 2002 the Later twins discovered that the process of painting and composing is almost identical. Anne-Fieke is a fine art painter and Eugène a composer. They share the same method of working and creative ideas, and as such it was a logical step to enter this process together. Creating pieces alongside each other, in order to come to a new expression of art: Tweekunst (trnsl. Twinart). The project The Tobias symphony part 1 & 2 shows the synergy between painting and composing. Painting and music went hand in hand, simultaneously growing towards one whole.

Andy Summers (The Police)

The recordings of the music came into being under close cooperation with some outstanding musicians. One of them is Andy Summers, guitarist of the legendary band The Police. He is known for his unique play and sound. On the Tobias symphony he opens part 2 of the symphony with a beautiful lyrical guitar solo of 3 minutes.

Wiek Hijmans

Wiek Hijmans has been featured at the Holland Festival´s Night of the electric guitar 2003, at the Concertgebouw, Amsterdam, as 'the specialist in contemporary composed music for electric guitar'. In New York he received the Andres Segovia award for outstanding guitar playing. On the Tobias symphony he plays on his Gretsch (1968) a magical solo full of imagination.

The Tobias symphony is composed and arranged by Eugène Later.

The Tobias Symphony part 2 · Oil on panel

IMAGINAIRE VII 113

CLAUDE VERLINDE

1927 France
www.claude-verlinde.fr

Le Duo · Oil on panel

La Gorgone · Oil on panel

Le Rideau · Oil on panel

IMAGINAIRE VII

CAS WATERMAN
1958 The Netherlands
www.caswaterman.com

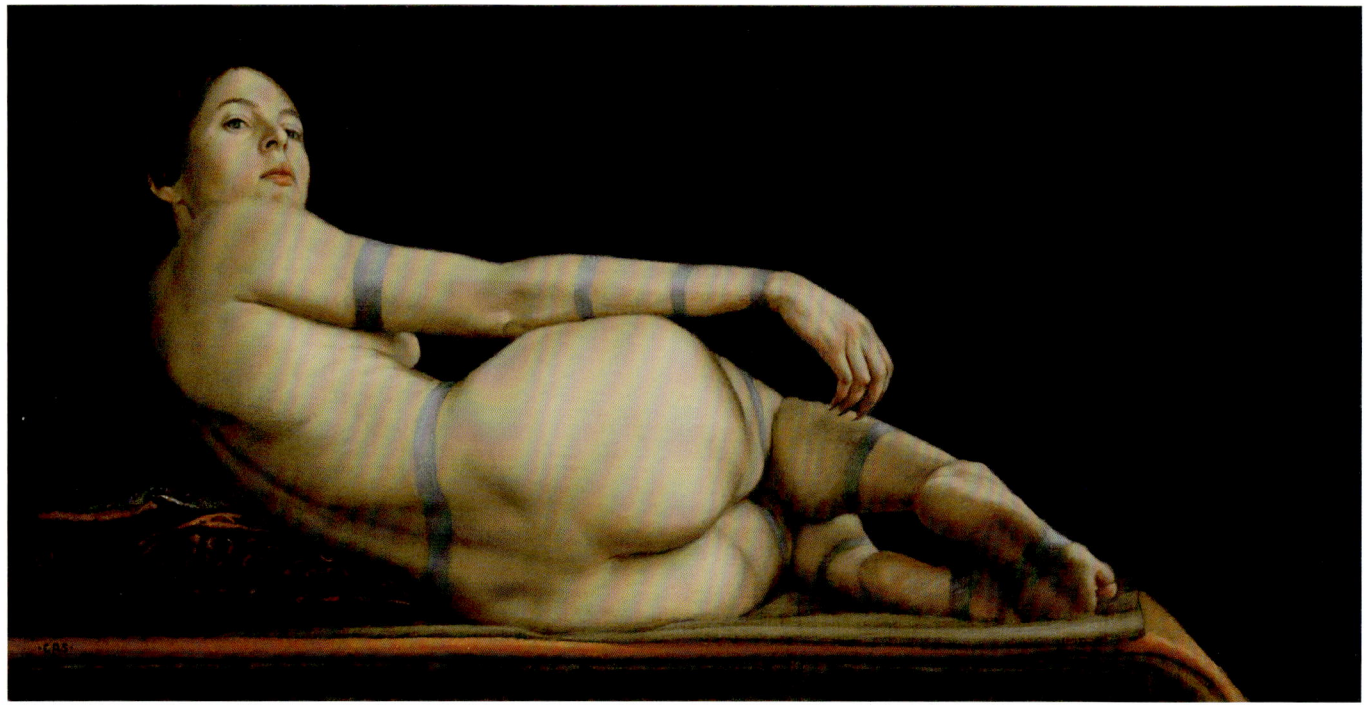

Tigermother · Oil on panel

On the Street · Oil on panel

STIG WEYE
1946 Denmark
www.stigweye.dk

No title · Acrylic on canvas

No title · Acrylic on canvas

No title · Acrylic on canvas

Photos: Jan Friis

IMAGINAIRE VII

DIRKJE WIGARDA
1963 The Netherlands
www.atelieramethyst.com

De toeschouwer · 30 x 24 cm - Oil on panel

De ontdekkingsreis · 20 x 8 cm · Oil on panel

My Dream · 24 x 18 cm · Oil on panel

Goddelijke kracht · 62 x 42 cm · Oil on panel

De overwintering · 19 x 7 cm · Oil on panel

IMAGINAIRE VII 121

SIEGFRIED ZADEMACK
1952 Germany
www.zademack.com

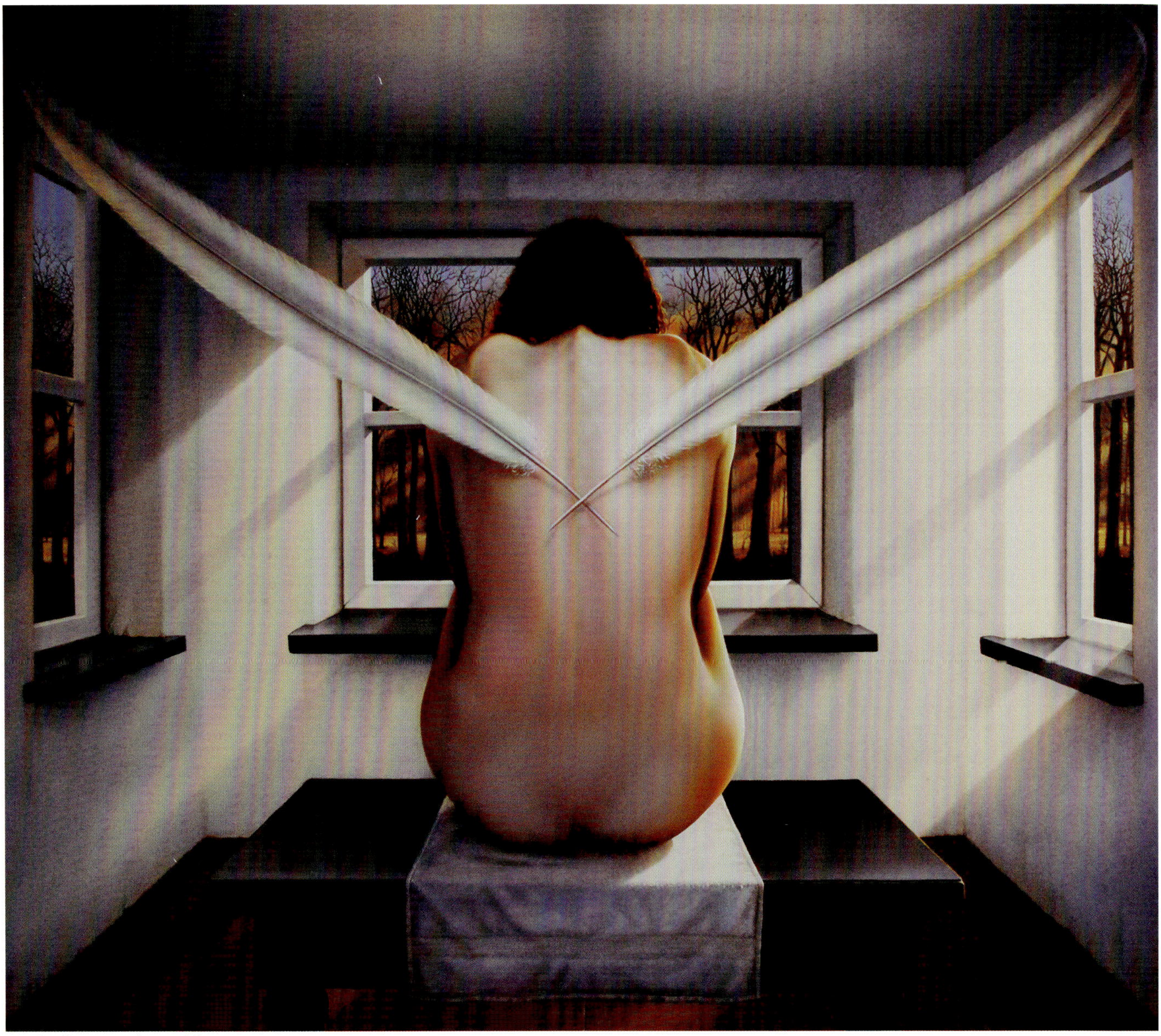

View Inside · 120 x 140 cm · Oil on canvas

Topless on the Beach · 80 x 40 cm · Oil on canvas

9 Bunnies on 15 Apples · Glazed stoneware

WINNIE STRØM SCHILDKNECHT
1973 Denmark
www.schildknecht.dk

Tweet Tweet · Glazed stoneware

Singing in the Rain · Bronze

Here comes the rain · Bronze

WINNIE STRØM SCHILDKNECHT
1973 Denmark
www.schildknecht.dk

Tweet Tweet · Glazed stoneware

Singing in the Rain · Bronze

Here comes the rain · Bronze

IMAGINAIRE VII 27

TIM ROOSEN

1972 Belgium
www.timroosen.be

Kadesh · Steel and copper · Lifesize

The Little Mermaid - The Prophecy of the Sea Witch · Bronze

Hand Kiss · Bronze

Bukken og Bruden · Bronze

HELLE RASK CRAWFORD
1964 Denmark
www.helleraskcrawford.dk

On the Edge · Bronze

Gate of Dreams · Bronze

Temptation Bronze

Sagittarius· Bronze

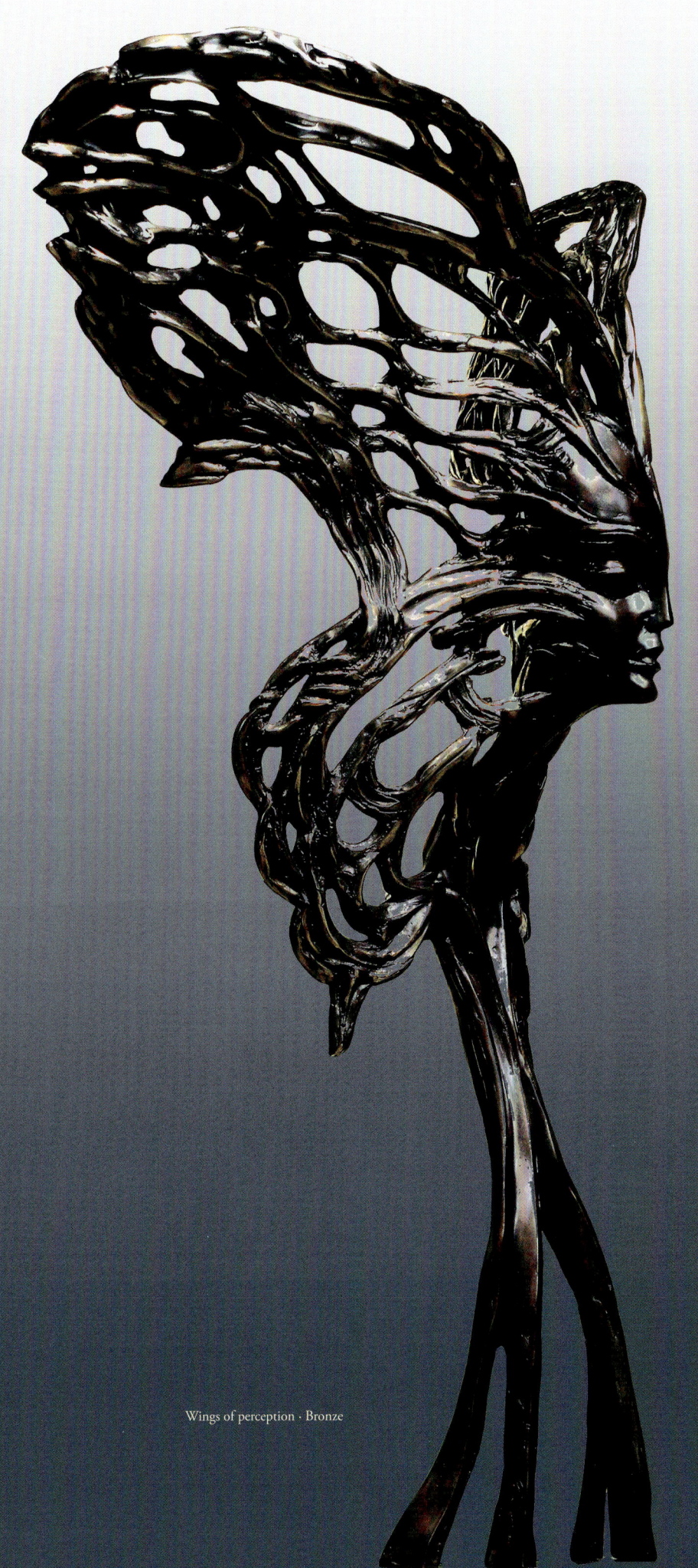

Wings of perception · Bronze

Rhino · Bronze

Hand of Luck · Bronze

Venice · Bronze

Dreamer · Bronze

Midnight Window - fragment · Bronze

Fragment of Touch of Imagination - 75 cm - Bronze

Touch of Imagination - 75 cm - Bronze

Lady of the Sea · Bronze

Lady Scorpio · Bronze

Night Flight · Bronze

Inner Vision · Bronze

Bull Thinker - Bronze

Violette Soul - Bronze

Midnight Window · Bronze

Beatrice · Bronze

IGOR GRECHANYK
1960 Ukraine
www.grechanyk.com

"Art of Igor Grechanyk" by Gerrit Luidinga

Igor Grechanyk is mesmerized by the mystery of the universe and regards it as his mission to make visible what is concealed beneath the surface of the phenomena, thus creating new worlds, so that spiritual energy is released. His creative work leads him in search of civilisations that are many thousands of years old.

In his quest he uses a method that has developed naturally. His unique and strictly idiosyncratic style is a logical consequence of his working method. The desire to shape is dependent on the expressive drive.

A sculpture arises from an idea that heralds itself like a distant melody. Initially abstract, it seeks to be captured in a form which slowly but surely manifests itself, not seldom to the surprise of the artist who goes into some sort of trance while working, often influenced by music that helps him to blend with the atmosphere of the work. The sculpture is thus born in a well-nigh organic manner, apparently without the maker's volition. This impression is deceptive, though, for there are forces at work in his subconscious directing his hands. The end result has the quality of a revelation, as soon as he leaves the work at rest and considers it from a distance. In a sense, Igor Grechanyk's artistry is a form of magic whose sole purpose it is to grant visibility to the invisible. In his objects the typical features of the subject have been laid down, the spirit has settled in them.

The artist himself links his working method to magic by referring to a specific characteristic of bronze which he compares to the alchemistic Philosopher's Stone, a substance thought to be capable of turning base metals into gold. The Swiss psychologist Carl Jung interpreted this quest for gold as manifestations of the unconscious. Which is how Igor Grechanyk sees it as well. In his own words: 'For me, bronze for my sculpture is not only the alloy of certain components in certain proportions, this is joining metal with the intention of the artist, this is a supernatural (or superartistic) act of the birth of Galatea.'

In fact, Igor Grechanyk's sculptures may be seen as symbols of a spiritual entity. His art shows a strong affinity with Symbolism, which, as a reaction to the realism that dominated the arts around 1850, focused attention on the power of imagination, fantastic images and intuition. Characteristic at that time were a strong yearning for the past and a focus on the subconscious, the mystery of the unusual and the inexplicable. Likewise Igor. He finds his inspiration in an older world which is very much alive in this day and age. It is the magic world of the mythologies of classical antiquity, Egypt, the Scythians and Christianity.

This is by no means exceptional. Within today's fantastic realism, too, many artists hark back to this past, in search of a reality that rises beyond the material as if in a new, modern Baroque which adds a dimension of weightlessness and incorporeality to the earthly dimensions. This pursuit is as old as humanity, among artists in particular.

In essence each genuine artist is an alchemist who wants to see anything he touches turn into gold. Like any genuine alchemist he will not desist from converting this pursuit into lifelong vigour with untiring efforts and full conviction. Igor Grechanyk is such an artist.

Apart from various solo exhibitions at different locations in Europe and beyond, he collaborates on a regular basis with the Galerie Alexander E. Raeber in Zürich, Switzerland and P&C Art Gallery in Washington DC, USA. Internationally he has made a name for himself. Over the years he completed several significant commissions for monuments in public areas, such as two sculptures of the Ukrainian poet Taras Shevchenko in Baku and Sofia and in Kiev a monument in honour of the bond of friendship between Kiev and Moscow. Furthermore his sculptures are part of the collection of several museums:

Academy of Art of Russian Federation, Fund of Ministry of Culture of Ukraine, Ukrainian Museum in New York, Ukrainian Institute of America, Museum of Spiritual Treasures of Ukraine in Kiev.

Metaphysics of Sound · 88 cm· Bronze

INDEX SCULPTORS

Page 6
IGOR GRECHANYK - GUEST OF HONOUR
Page 24
HELLE RASK CRAWFORD
Page 26
TIM ROOSEN
Page 28
WINNIE STRØM SCHILDKNECHT

IMAGINAIRE VII

Contemporary Magic Realism

First published in Denmark 2014
Copyright © 2014 Edition Brusen - FBB-FANTASMUS Bisgaard Brusen - FANTASMUS Artbooks

First edition

All rights reserved to the publisher. No part of this book may be reproduced or transmitted in any form, mannor or media including photography, recording or any other information storage and retrieval system, nor may pages be applied to any material, cut, trimmed or sized to alter the excisting trim sizes (or) matted or framed with the intent to create other products for sale or resale or profit in any manor whatsoever, withour prior permission in writing from the publisher and/or the artists.

IMAGINAIRE VII
2014, with reg.
ISBN: 978-87-993936-6-4
EAN: 9788799393664
ISSN: 1903-7708

Introduction by Claus Brusen
FANTASMUS - Since then - Now - Coming up by Mette Torp Bisgaard

Special thanks to Steven Kenny and Igor Grechanyk
Set in Adobe Garamond Pro
Design and Layout by Mette Torp Bisgaard, FANTASMUS

Cover: Steven Kenny, The Ruff, Oil on panel
Flipsidecover: Igor Grechanyk, Nihgt Fly, Bronze
Inside cover: Michael Maschka, Hoffnung auf Frieden, Oil on panel

www.fantasmus.com

IMAGINAIRE
The Magic Seven

Contemporary Magic Realism

www.fantasmus.com